ROMANTIC ROYAL MARRIAGES

ROMANTIC ROYAL MARRIAGES

BARBARA CARTLAND

BEAUFORT BOOKS

NEW YORK · TORONTO

Other Books by Barbara Cartland

ROMANTIC NOVELS
Over 300, the most recently
published being:

The Waltz of Hearts
Dollars for the Duke
Dreams Do Come True
A Night of Gaiety
Count the Stars
Winged Magic
A Portrait of Love
River of Love
Gift of the Gods
The Heart of the Clan
An Innocent in Russia
A Shaft of Sunlight
Love Wins
Enchanted
The Wings of Ecstasy
Pure and Untouched
In the Arms of Love
Touch a Star
For All Eternity
Secret Harbour

The Dream and the Glory
(in aid of the St John Ambulance
Brigade)

AUTOBIOGRAPHICAL AND BIOGRAPHICAL

The Isthmus Years, 1919–1939
The Years of Opportunity, 1939–1945
I Search for Rainbows, 1945–1976
We Danced All Night, 1919–1929
Ronald Cartland (with a Foreword by
Sir Winston Churchill)
Polly My Wonderful Mother
I Seek the Miraculous

HISTORICAL

Bewitching Women
*The Outrageous Queen (The Story of
Queen Christina of Sweden)*
The Scandalous Life of King Carol
*The Private Life of Elizabeth, Empress of
Austria*

Josephine, Empress of France
Diane de Poitiers
Metternich – the Passionate Diplomat

SOCIOLOGY

You in the Home
The Fascinating Forties
Marriage for Moderns
Be Vivid, Be Vital
Love, Life and Sex
Vitamins for Vitality
Husbands and Wives
Etiquette
The Many Facets of Love
Sex and the Teenager
The Book of Charm
Living Together
The Youth Secret
The Magic of Honey
*Barbara Cartland's Book of Beauty and
Health*
Men are Wonderful

COOKERY

*Barbara Cartland's Health Food Cookery
Book*
Food for Love
Magic of Honey Cookbook
Recipes for Lovers

EDITOR OF

The Common Problems by Ronald
Cartland (with a preface by the
Rt. Hon. the Earl of Selborne, P.C.)
Barbara Cartland's Library of Love
*Barbara Cartland's Library of Ancient
Wisdom*

DRAMA

Blood Money
French Dressing

PHILOSOPHY

Touch the Stars

RADIO OPERETTA

The Rose and the Violet (music by Mark
Lubbock), performed in 1942

RADIO PLAYS

*The Caged Bird: An Episode in the Life of
Elizabeth Empress of Austria,*
performed in 1957

GENERAL

*Barbara Cartland's Book of Useless
Information*, with a Foreword by The
Earl Mountbatten of Burma (in aid
of the United World Colleges)
Love and Lovers (Picture Book)
The Light of Love (Prayer Book)
Barbara Cartland's Scrapbook, in aid of
the Royal Photographic Museum

VERSE

Lines on Life and Love

MUSIC

An Album of Love Songs sung with the
Royal Philharmonic Orchestra

MAGAZINE

Barbara Cartland's World of Romance
(published in the USA)

SPECIAL PUBLICATION

Love at the Helm, inspired and helped
by Admiral of the Fleet Earl
Mountbatten of Burma, in aid of the
Mountbatten Memorial Trust

Published in the United States of America by Beaufort Books Inc., New York and Toronto

First published 1981

Published simultaneously in England by Express Newspapers Ltd
Published simultaneously in Canada by General Publishing Co. Ltd

Designed and produced for Beaufort Books Inc by Bellew & Higton Publishers Ltd,
19–21 Conway Street, London W1P 6JD

Copyright © Barbara Cartland 1981

ISBN 0-8253-0076-2

Computerset by MFK Graphic Systems (Typesetting) Ltd, Saffron Walden, Essex

Printed and bound in England by The Artisan Press Ltd, Beaumont Leys, Leicester, England

CONTENTS

1	HM King William, the Conqueror, & Matilda of Flanders	8
2	HM King John & Isabella of Aquitaine	10
3	HM King Edward I & Eleanor of Castile	12
4	HM Mary, Queen of France, & the Duke of Suffolk	14
5	HM King Henry VIII & Anne Boleyn	16
6	HM Mary, Queen of Scots, & the Earl of Darnley	18
7	Shah Jehan, Emperor of India, & Begum Mumtaz Mahal	20
8	HM King Louis XIV & Madame de Maintenon	22
9	HRH Prince Augustus of Saxony & Archduchess Maria Josepha of Hungary and Bohemia	25
10	HSH Prince Honoré III of Monaco & Catherine de Brignole	26
11	Catherine the Great, Empress of Russia, & Prince Gregory Potemkin	27
12	Sultan Abd ul Hamid of Turkey & Mademoiselle Aimée Dubucq	28
13	HRH The Prince of Wales & Mrs Maria FitzHerbert	30
14	HRH Prince Augustus, Duke of Sussex, & the Lady Augusta Murray	34
15	Napoleon Bonaparte, Emperor of France, & Josephine de Beauharnais	36
16	Joachim Murat & Caroline Bonaparte, King and Queen of Naples	38
17	HRH Princess Charlotte of Great Britain & HH Prince Leopold of Saxe-Coburg	40
18	HCM Maria Cristina, Queen Regent of Spain, & Don Augustin Fernando Muñoz y Sanchez	42
19	HH Prince Ferdinand of Saxe-Coburg & HRH Dona Maria da Gloria	44
20	HM Queen Victoria of Great Britain & HH Prince Albert of Saxe-Coburg and Gotha	46
21	HRH Prince George, Duke of Cambridge, & Miss Louisa Fairbrother	49
22	HH Prince Alexander of Hesse and the Rhine & Julie, Countess von Hauke	50
23	HIM Napoleon III & Eugénie de Montijo	52
24	HI & RH Franz Joseph, Emperor of Austria, & Elisabeth, Duchess in Bavaria	54
25	Sheik Abdul Medjuel el Mezrab & Miss Jane Digby	56
26	HM King George I of Greece & HIH Grand Duchess Olga of Russia	58
27	HRH Prince Frederick of Denmark & HRH Princess Louise of Sweden and Norway	59
28	Prince Si Ahmed Tedjani & Mademoiselle Aurélie Piccard	60
29	HCM King Alfonso XII of Spain & Dona Maria de las Mercedes	62
30	Tsar Alexander II & Princess Catherine Dolgornky	64
31	HM King Alexander I of Bulgaria & Miss Louise Loisinger	66
32	HSH Prince Albert I of Monaco & the Duchesse de Richelieu	67
33	HRH Prince George, Duke of York & HH Princess May of Teck	68
34	Tsar Nicholas II & HH Princess Alix of Hesse and Darmstadt	70
35	HRH Crown Princess Louise of Saxony & Signor Enrico Toselli	73
36	HRH Prince Ernst August of Hanover & HRH Princess Viktoria Luise of Prussia	74
37	HH Princess Indira of Baroda & HH Maharaja of Cooch Behar	76
38	HM King Alexander of Greece & Aspasia Manos	76
39	HRH Prince Albert, Duke of York & the Lady Elizabeth Bowes-Lyon	78
40	HRH Prince Paul of Yugoslavia & HRH Princess Olga of Greece	82
41	HRH Prince George, Duke of Kent & HRH Princess Marina of Greece	84
42	HM King Edward VIII & Mrs Wallis Simpson	86
43	HH Maharaja of Jaipur & HH Princess Ayesha of Cooch-Behar	88
44	HRH Princess Elizabeth & Lieutenant Philip Mountbatten	90
45	HM King Carol II of Roumania & Madame Elena Lupescu	94
46	HSH Prince Rainier III of Monaco & Grace Kelly	95
47	HM Baudouin, King of the Belgians, & Dona Fabiola Mora y Aragon	96
48	HRH Princess Margaret & Antony Armstrong-Jones	98
49	HRH Prince Edward, Duke of Kent, & Miss Katharine Worsley	100
50	HRH Prince Juan Carlos of Spain & HRH Princess Sofia of Greece	102
51	HM Maharaj-Prince Sikkim Palden Thondup Namgyal & Miss Hope Cooke	103
52	HRH Princess Alexandra of Kent & the Hon. Angus Ogilvy	104
53	HRH Crown Princess Beatrix of the Netherlands & Claus von Amsberg	106
54	HRH Princess Margrethe of Denmark & Count Henry de Laborde de Monpezat	108
55	HRH Crown Prince Harald of Norway & Miss Sonja Haraldsen	110
56	HRH Princess Anne & Captain Mark Phillips	112
57	HM King Leka I of Albania & Miss Susan Cullen-Ward	116
58	HM King Carl XVI Gustaf of Sweden & Miss Silvia Sommerlath	118
59	HRH Prince Michael of Kent & Baroness Marie-Christine von Reibnitz	120
60	HRH The Prince of Wales & the Lady Diana Spencer	122

About the Author

Barbara Cartland, the world's most famous romantic novelist, who is also an historian, playwright, lecturer, political speaker and television personality, has now sold over 200 million books throughout the world. Her 300th book, a novel, will be published on her 80th birthday.

She has also had many historical works published and has written four autobiographies as well as the biographies of her mother and that of her brother, Ronald Cartland, who was the first Member of Parliament to be killed in the last war. This book has a preface by Sir Winston Churchill and has just been republished with an introduction by Sir Arthur Bryant.

She has recently completed a novel, *Love at the Helm*, with the help and inspiration of the late Admiral of the Fleet, the Earl Mountbatten of Burma. This is being sold for the Mountbatten Memorial Trust.

Miss Cartland in 1978 sang *An Album of Love Songs* with the Royal Philharmonic Orchestra.

In 1976, by writing twenty-one books, she broke the world record and has continued for the following four years with twenty-four, twenty, twenty-three and twenty-four. In the *Guinness Book of Records* she is listed as the world's top-selling author.

In private life Barbara Cartland, who is a Dame of the Order of St John of Jerusalem, Chairman of the St John Council in Hertfordshire and Deputy President of the St John Ambulance Brigade, has fought for better conditions and salaries for Midwives and Nurses.

She has championed the cause for old people, had the law altered regarding gypsies and founded the first Romany gypsy camp in the world.

Barbara Cartland is deeply interested in Vitamin Therapy and is President of the National Association for Health.

She has a magazine, *Barbara Cartland's World of Romance*, now being published in the USA and 'Barbara Cartland's Romantic World Tours' operate from America in conjunction with British Airways.

INTRODUCTION

It is generally supposed that until this century and after the First World War, all Royal Marriages were arranged for political or national motives.

These included the acquisition of territory and the optimistic hope that the linking of two Ruling houses would ensure peace for the peoples over whom they ruled.

Ninety-nine people out of a hundred were also sure that when Lady Elizabeth Bowes-Lyon, now our beloved Queen Mother, married the Duke of York, later George VI, it was the first love-match in Britain.

I have therefore found it fascinating to discover that the first English King to marry for love was William the Conqueror. Far more Royalty in Europe have made love-matches than anyone had ever imagined. I do hope you enjoy reading about some of them.

HM KING WILLIAM I, THE CONQUEROR,
& MATILDA OF FLANDERS
1053

14th-century Manuscript showing William the Conqueror with his troops and baggage.

William's ships. Were the men or the horses most seasick?

English monarchs in 1066 were not chosen by heredity, but any great nobleman who had some Royal blood in his veins could stake his claim.

Duke William II of Normandy, was illegitimate, and the only relationship to the early English Kings was that he was a great-nephew of Queen Emma, mother by her first husband to Edward the Confessor.

William was under forty when he invaded England, but he was an extremely experienced ruler, administrator and commander, having been for twenty years in charge of his own Duchy. This he had inherited from his great-grandfather Duke Rollo of Normandy.

Among the descendants of Duke Rollo, especially through the Granvilles, are many of the greatest families in Great Britain – Lansdowne, Bath, Sutherland, Dysart, and the Earls Spencer. They, therefore, through this line, are related to Ethelred the Unready, Edward the Confessor, King Canute and William the Conqueror.

had three horses killed under him and he was crowned in Westminster Abbey. He had negotiated in 1051 a marriage with Matilda, daughter of Count Baldwin V of Flanders.

Matilda at first refused to consider marrying 'a bastard'. She was tiny (only four feet tall), well-educated, beautiful – and William had no intention of being 'refused'.

He set upon Matilda one day when she came out of Church; he tore her rich clothes, kicked her, flung her down in the street and, in modern parlance, 'beat her up'. At the time she was sixteen and he was twenty.

Like women all through the ages Matilda was thrilled to be conquered by a masterful man. She accepted him, but they waited five years to be married – with great pomp. They had a very happy marriage and she was crowned in 1068 at Winchester. She was the first real Queen of England.

William was entirely faithful to Matilda, which was unusual in those days. He trusted her implicitly and allowed her to share all his glories.

They had four sons and several daughters but it may have been due to Matilda's influence that in William's laws for keeping order was one which said: *'If a man lie with a woman against her will, he is forthwith condemned to forfeit those members with which he has desported himself.'*

William showed the Anglo-Saxon nobles how a

William victorious, he conquered Matilda, but she held him captive with her love.

King should live. At Christmas, Easter and Whitsun he put on a calculated display of magnificence and offered delicacies of food from Constantinople, Babylon, Tripoli, Syria and Phoenicia.

The Norman Court set new standards of social behaviour and a new elegance.

Close to death in 1087, William said in a prayer: 'I commend myself to Mary, the Holy Mother of God, my Heavenly mistress, that by Her Blessed intercession, I may be reconciled to Her Beloved Son, Our Lord Jesus Christ.'

After that he died instantly.

HM KING JOHN & ISABELLA OF AQUITAINE
1200

King John. Judicious, extortionate, grasping, generous, astute, reckless!

Queen Isabella. Beautiful and understanding even her husband's frequent infidelity.

John was the youngest child of Henry Plantagenet and Eleanor, Duchess of Aquitaine, a great heiress. He was born when his mother was forty-five and was destined for the Church.

At the age of nine he was betrothed to his infant cousin Isobelle of Gloucester, but it was just a political agreement and John managed to get out of it on the plea that it was illegal because of their close relationship.

He continued to be friendly with Isobelle, and for the rest of his life sent her presents of cloth, wine and sugar. Finally he married her to the Earl of Essex, who had to pay 20,000 marks for her.

Then at the moment of John's accession in 1200 he fell passionately in love.

Isabella, daughter of Count Audemar of Angoulême in Aquitaine, was only twelve. She was also engaged to the widowed Hugh IX, Lord

King John stag-hunting. A sportsman, he also loved luxury.

of Lusignan, Count of La Marche. John, however, swept Isabella into his arms, carried her across the Channel to England, and in 1200 they were crowned together at Westminster.

They devoted the next six months to travelling round England, visiting York and spending Easter at Canterbury, where they 'wore their crowns'.

Hugh Le Brun was furious that his bride-to-be should have been abducted, however willingly. He started a war which resulted in John losing nearly all his Continental possessions.

John had two sons and three daughters with Isabella, as well as five illegitimate children.

John was short, dark and proud. He liked comfort – especially baths, which he took frequently. He loved jewellery and had a famous collection. Among the pieces lost in the quicksands of the Wash was the regalia worn by his grandmother Matilda when she was crowned Empress.

He spent much time hunting, and liked food and wine. He was very partial to eggs, of which he ordered five thousand for his Christmas festivities in 1206.

The stories that he was cruel and worse than his contemporaries have no basis in fact. The hot temper of the Angevins was notorious and the legends of the time said they were descended from the Devil. But John was a good soldier and a hard-working and conscientious Civil administrator. He died in 1216.

HM KING EDWARD I & ELEANOR OF CASTILE
1254

Queen Eleanor. Her ecstatic love has survived the centuries of Time.

King Edward worshipped Eleanor and never recovered from her death.

The effigy of Eleanor of Castile in Westminster Abbey is one of the earliest as well as one of the most beautiful of England's Queens.

When Eleanor died of a 'slow fever' in 1290, her husband Edward I ordered 'Eleanor Crosses' for the twelve places at which her coffin had rested on its long journey from Harby in Nottinghamshire to Westminster. She lies with her hair flowing on to her shoulders, wearing an open crown of fleur-de-lys finials.

Eleanor was adored by the King and they were so happy together they could not bear to be parted, so she accompanied him on a Crusade.

There is a legend that when he was wounded by a Saracen assassin, she sucked the poison from his arm. Whether this is true or not, she was so distressed when the septic wound was dressed that Edward had to tell his brother-in-law and a trusted knight to carry her from his tent.

Edward I was a man of real ability. Apart from his ambitions – and he was successful in striving for new territories in Wales, Scotland and Belgium – he was the true founder of the English Common Law and largely the designer of Parliament.

His son, later Edward II, was the first Prince of Wales.

The gilt-bronze effigy of Queen Eleanor in Westminster Abbey.

'Eleanor Cross' at Sledmore in Yorkshire.

'Eleanor Cross' at Hardingstone, Northamptonshire.

'Eleanor Cross' at Beddington, Northamptonshire.

HM MARY, QUEEN OF FRANCE, & THE DUKE OF SUFFOLK

1515

There was a national outcry in 1515 when it was learnt that Mary Tudor, the beautiful, young, exquisitely graceful sister of Henry VIII, was to marry toothless, broken-down Louis XII.

She had however consented to the alliance only when Henry promised that she could marry the Duke of Suffolk, whom she loved, as soon as Louis died. King Louis conveniently did so eleven weeks after the marriage.

However, Louis' lascivious nephew and successor Francis forced his attentions upon the beautiful widow. Another threat arose when Henry VIII wanted Mary to marry Archduke Charles, the ugliest and most powerful ruler in Europe.

'I would rather be torn in pieces,' Mary cried.

Suffolk tried to soothe her fears, but she threatened that unless he married her at once she would believe that he, too, was forcing the Archduke on her.

At this, Suffolk, who adored her, cast prudence to the winds and married her secretly, knowing he might be beheaded.

Henry was furious, but Mary was his favourite sister and by the time the two lovers reached England his anger had cooled.

Their clandestine liaison was publicly solemnized at Greenwich on 13 May 1515 in the presence of the King and the entire Court.

The marriage of Mary Tudor in 1514 to the toothless, aged, dissolute King Louis XII of France, illustrated by an eye-witness of the Wedding Ceremony.

Mary Tudor, the sister of King Henry VIII. 'A nymph from Heaven ... a paradise' was how the Venetian Ambassador described her.

The Duke of Suffolk was a hearty, handsome man enviously adored for his amorous achievements by his friend the King.

HM KING HENRY VIII & ANNE BOLEYN
1533

Henry VIII, ruthless, self-willed, accomplished, wildly energetic, musical, irresistibly passionate.

Anne Boleyn, dark, fascinating, beautiful black witch-like eyes.

When Henry VIII came to the throne he was described as 'the handsomest sovereign in Christendom' with a fine calf to his leg, auburn hair and 'a round face so beautiful it would become a pretty woman'.

He was also accomplished in speaking French, Spanish, Latin and a little Italian. He played well on the lute and harpsichord and jousted 'magnificently'.

He married Katharine of Aragon in 1509, and it seemed at first to be a most successful marriage, but their son, the Prince of Wales, died when he was two months old and Henry was heartbroken.

By 1520 Henry no longer cared for Katharine who, wrinkled and dumpy, was approaching forty. What is more, four sons had died at birth or been stillborn and only a girl, Mary, had survived.

Henry began to look for an excuse to be rid of Katharine, and in the meantime he fell in love.

Anne Boleyn was accused of being a witch in league with the devil. Certainly her black and beautiful eyes held him enthralled.

The Boleyns were rich merchants, but Anne's sister Mary had been Henry's mistress and Anne became lady-in-waiting to Queen Katharine.

Henry openly declared his feelings for Anne, but, to his surprise and consternation, Anne returned to her father's home.

The King hated writing letters, but suddenly he was perpetually scribbling out love letters for Royal messengers to carry to Kent.

'I presume I shall take you alone for my mistress, cast all others out of my thoughts and affections and serve you only,' he wrote.

Anne sent back teasing replies: she had no intention of being his mistress. The King approached Rome for the annulment of his marriage.

Anne Boleyn kept the King enthralled for six frustrating years.

After six years Anne was bored with waiting and being just the King's companion. He created her *Marquis* of Pembroke with precedence over all other *Marquises*, but it was not enough.

It required an iron determination and a witch's wiles to keep the King in a fever-pitch of passion – desiring her, pleading with her, commanding her – yet still refuse to be his mistress.

He wanted her and, God knows, she wanted to be his wife.

Pressed by the King, who was pressed by Anne, in 1533 the Archbishop of Canterbury defied Rome and declared that Henry and Katharine had never been husband and wife! Within a week Anne Boleyn was crowned Queen.

A daughter was born to Anne in 1533 and christened Elizabeth. Two years later, Queen Katharine died. Henry and Anne celebrated. Dressed from head to foot in yellow, they went to Mass and had a banquet, after which there was dancing and jousting.

But as the deposed Queen was buried Anne miscarried. It was the beginning of the end. Henry fell in love with one of her Ladies-in-Waiting. On 19 May 1536 Anne went to the block.

Hever Castle, Anne's home where she received passionately entreating letters.

HM MARY, QUEEN OF SCOTS, & THE EARL OF DARNLEY

1565

Mary Queen of Scots and her second husband the Earl of Darnley. She was elegant, graceful, coquettish, passionate, brave, intelligent and impetuous. Darnley was spoilt, conceited, touchy, boastful and ambitious.

The Earl of Bothwell, proud, vicious and vainglorious, placed the Queen in a situation in which she was obliged to marry him. He abducted and ravished her, it is popularly believed against her will.

He looks like a young god and he is the properest and best proportioned man I have ever seen,' Queen Mary said the first time she met the Earl of Darnley. When they danced together she found him even more attractive.

Queen Elizabeth was using Mary's unmarried state as an argument for not recognizing her place in the English succession, and the idea of 'the fair, jolly young man' as a husband was very enticing to Mary.

Besides, he wooed her with poetry, with words, and with vibrations of passion which matched her own.

Mary's feelings for Darnley were overwhelmingly physical. In the years since the death of her first husband, François, the Dauphin of France, she had led a life of celibacy, and the tumultuous emotions aroused by Darnley swept over her like a flood-tide.

Her infatuation grew until it was whispered that Darnley had bewitched her, while his overwhelming arrogance daily increased his detractors and enemies.

While they waited for Papal approval Darnley contracted measles; while she was in and out of his sickroom Mary's love became so explosive that they were secretly married by a priest introduced into the Castle by Mary's Italian teacher, Rizzio.

At last on 22 July 1565 Darnley was made Duke of Albany and a week later they were married publicly.

Darnley, more puffed up with his importance than ever, treated his wife abominably, and she began to rely on the friendship and advice of Rizzio.

On 9 March 1566 he was dragged shrieking from her supper table by a crowd of angry nobles led by Darnley, stabbed fifty times and thrown out of the window into the courtyard.

After her husband's treachery Mary loathed him. But first their son must be born, and while she bided her time she fell in love with the Earl of Bothwell.

Luring Darnley into a false sense of security, she nursed him through an illness and everyone in Edinburgh believed that the Queen and Darnley were once again a loving couple.

A year after Rizzio's death on Sunday 9 February 1567, a high festival was held in the Palace of Holyrood, but Darnley was sleeping at Kirk o'Field, a lonely, isolated house chosen by Bothwell. The Queen was however staying at the Palace.

Queen Mary and Darnley 'balling, dancing and banquetting'.

At two o'clock in the morning a thunderous explosion completely destroyed the house in Kirk o'Field.

The corpses of Darnley and his servant, who slept in his room, were found in the garden clad only in their shirts.

Mary's carnal marriage 'began with happiness – ended in strife'.

19

SHAH JEHAN, EMPEROR OF INDIA, & BEGUM MUMTAZ MAHAL

1612

After Mumtaz Mahal died, every day for the next twenty-two years Shah Jehan set 20,000 men to work on her tomb. Its brick scaffolding cost £9 million and the building itself more than £18 million before it was finished in 1653. Vast, in Mogul-style concept, it was furnished like a jewel-box.

In 1617 Shah Jehan was ill and his son Aurengzeb imprisoned his father. To send him mad he sent him another son's severed head and for seven years ordered troops to fire muskets and beat drums all night outside his prison. Shah Jehan finally died from an overdose of aphrodisiacs when he saw two concubines in a mirror mocking his virility.

Shah Jehan, who was the Mogul Emperor of India from 1628 to 1658, loved architecture and jewels. He usually wore £4,000,000's worth and stored another £6,000,000.

He married in 1612 the beautiful Begum Mumtaz Muhal, whom he loved passionately. She was his constant companion and went with him everywhere for thirty-one years. She helped and inspired him to build the amazing immortal monuments of the Mogul age.

The Hall of private audience in the Red Fort at Delhi had walls of precious stones bedded in marble, a ceiling of beaten silver and a Peacock Throne of solid gold.

The Pearl Mosque at Agra sent the spirit soaring in rapture.

The Shalimar Gardens in Kashmir were a dream of delight.

When the beloved Mumtaz Mahal died, aged thirty-nine, after the birth of her fourteenth child, Shah Jehan was broken-hearted. He set 20,000 men to work on her tomb and when the Taj Mahal (a play on her name) was finished it was, and still is, one of the Wonders of the World.

No woman has ever had a more exquisite memorial, erected to commemorate a great and enduring love. To see it lifts the heart with the ecstasy which only love can give.

HM KING LOUIS XIV, THE SUN KING, & MADAME DE MAINTENON

1683

She was a widow, certainly a virgin, pious and ladylike.

The Queen died in the arms of Mme de Maintenon. 'Poor woman,' the King said, 'it's the only time she gave me any trouble.' Mme de Maintenon was given rooms in the Queen's Suite.

Madame de Maintenon started her Royal career by being governess to the King's illegitimate children. In 1674 she began what she called her 'long struggle for the King's soul'.

Mistress after mistress appeared but the King was at ease with Madame. She was beautiful, with brilliant blue eyes, a widow, and she amused him. It was a pleasure every time she opened her mouth! Finally he loved her.

No one knew exactly when they were married in the autumn of 1683: Madame de Maintenon burnt all relevant documents after the King's death, but it must have been at Versailles in the little oratory in the King's apartment. The King now addressed her as 'Madame', as he had the Queen.

In 1702, when Madame was sixty-seven, she wrote to the Bishop of Chartres saying she was extremely tired and asking whether she could now refuse to go to bed with the King twice a day. 'These painful occasions', she said, were now too much for her.

The Bishop replied that she must obey her husband's wishes.

Madame de Maintenon had a conflicting nature and often wished she was dead.

After her marriage she hardly ever left her own appartments to mingle with society and the few who were received in her room found themselves in the presence of the Queen!

She prided herself on wearing no jewels but the cross which dangled from a necklace of huge perfectly matched pearls was set with the finest diamonds in the King's collection.

HRH Prince Augustus of Saxony & Archduchess Maria Josepha of Hungary and Bohemia

1719

Augustus of Saxony was the son of Augustus the Strong – a man of great taste who made Dresden the most civilized city in the world and had a harem of lovely women. Augustus was more interested in pictures than power and his passion for the arts was even greater than his father's.

But though he adored beauty he fell madly in love with the clever, fascinating – but excessively plain, almost dwarfish – Archduchess Maria Josepha, and married her in 1719 in Vienna.

When Augustus the Strong died he left 354 bastards.

When the happy pair arrived in Dresden, his father mistook a very pretty Lady-in-Waiting for the bride and kissed her with paternal fervour.

After the mistake had been pointed out to him, Augustus the Strong consoled the pretty Lady-in-Waiting for not being his daughter-in-law by making her his mistress.

HSH Prince Honoré III of Monaco
& Catherine de Brignole
1757

Honoré III was determined, unlike his predecessors, to marry for love. He had lost his heart to Catherine de Brignole, daughter of the former Doge of Genoa.

However, the marriage, after a great deal of planning, was very nearly cancelled at the last moment by the bride's mother.

Having arrived from Genoa with Catherine in a galley, she insisted that the bridegroom come aboard to collect her. Honoré, however, as a

Alas, their love only lasted for three years.

Sovereign, refused to advance further than the landing stage.

The Genoese flotilla turned round and sailed back to Bordighera. It returned two days later only because the bride's uncle, moved by her tears, found a solution to the problem. A bridge of boats was built between the shore and the galley and the young couple met half way!

Mrs FitzHerbert who at the age of seventeen was married to a wealthy, middle-aged landowner who died in a year. Graceful, with a nose too long, a fine bosom and lovely dark brown eyes, she was a good listener.

Herbert were secretly married at her house, with her uncle and brother as witnesses. The Prince and Maria, husband and wife in the sight of God, but not by the law of the Realm, drove off that night for a brief honeymoon.

Together, separated, together, then Maria FitzHerbert passed out of the Prince's life. Yet he always considered her his true wife and when he died her miniature was found in a locket round his neck.

31

WIFE & no WIFE or A trip to the Continent.

Cartoon of the Secret Marriage between the Prince of Wales and Mrs FitzHerbert. James Fox is giving the Bride away while Lord North sleeps.

The truth was that on 15 December 1785 the Prince married Maria FitzHerbert secretly in her Drawing-Room, with her uncle and younger brother present, and immediately after they left for a short honeymoon.

The Prince of Pleasure when he grew older, and was 'The First Gentleman in Europe'. He had tremendous charm, was a clever mimic, an unerring judge of Art, and was wildly, hopelessly extravagant.

He bought everything in large quantities. Needing a walking-stick, he bought thirty-two in one day. The Prince was equally generous with his friends and family. One bill was for forty-eight pairs of women's fancy white silk hose!

The Prince's greatest extravagance, the Royal Pavilion at Brighton.

HRH Prince Augustus, Duke of Sussex, & The Lady Augusta Murray

1793

His Royal Highness Prince Augustus, Duke of Sussex, good-looking, good-tempered, passionately in love and abominably treated by his father.

Prince Augustus, the sixth son of King George III, fell madly in love with Lady Augusta Murray, aged thirty, when he was nineteen years old.

He was a handsome young man, but because he had 'convulsive asthma' he could not serve in the Army like his brothers. Instead he became something of a classical scholar and had a collection of 5000 Bibles. He had a fine singing voice and while living in Italy had practised music for eight hours a day.

Knowing that his marriage with Lady Augusta must be secret, as he would never obtain his

Lady Augusta Murray, desperately in love with the fascinating Prince, who was younger than herself, but she would not give herself to him, nor would he take her before they were married because their love was true and sacred.

The marriage of Prince Augustus Frederick with Lady Augusta Murray.

father's approval, the Prince found a clergyman called Gunn to marry them.

The Prince wrote to Lady Augusta, whom he called 'Goosy':

4th April 1793

Will you allow me to come this evening? It is my only hope. Oh! Let me come, and we will send for Mr Gunn. Everything but this is hateful to me. More than forty-eight hours have I passed without the slightest nourishment. Oh, let me not live so . . .

If Gunn will not marry me, I shall die.

They were married at St George's, Hanover Square on 24 November 1793, and in January a year later Augusta gave birth to a son at her parents' home.

The same month the King learnt of the marriage and His Majesty's action was swift and savage. He kept the Prince abroad and forbade his wife to join him, and they did not see each other for six years.

During this time the Prince wrote her despairing love letters while trying to placate the Arches Court of Canterbury, which, in the meantime, was declaring the marriage null, void and illegal, thereby making their son illegitimate. The Prince fought the decision every inch of the way.

The Prince and Augusta lived together for a few months in London, and she gave birth to a daughter in 1801.

Augusta died in 1829 and the Duke married Lady Cecilia Buggin, again secretly, and according to the Royal Marriage Act, illegally. She was very small, good-humoured and attractive.

Napoleon Bonaparte was ensnared by his wife.

He wrote: 'A thousand kisses as burning as you are cold.'

'... last night's delirium have robbed my senses of repose ... sweet incomparable Josephine, what an extraordinary influence you have over my heart ... accept a thousand kisses but give me none, for they fire my heart.'

Josephine was one of those fascinating women who are not beautiful but who are irresistible to men. After her first husband, the Vicomte de Beauharnais, was guillotined, she had several lovers, and at thirty-two years of age, shortly after she met General Bonaparte in 1795, she went to bed with him.

Napoleon was consumed with love. For the first time in his life he knew the real satisfaction of passion – given and received.

They became engaged but Josephine would not name the day. Then on Wednesday 8 March 1796, a stormy night, the Mayor of the district in which Napoleon lived was got out of bed by a man in the uniform of a General who told him to perform a marriage ceremony immediately.

The simple Civil union of the Revolutionary Regime was soon over. The bride and groom returned to Josephine's house and to the same bed where, in the past few weeks, they had already found happiness.

The Civil marriage of Napoleon and Josephine, after which they went back to bed.

The Coronation of Napoleon Bonaparte took place on 2 December 1804, at Notre-Dame. The Pope anointed Napoleon, who crowned himself and afterwards crowned Josephine. During the service Napoleon whispered to his brother Joseph: 'If our father could see us now!'

Josephine's glamorous but very narrow bed at Malmaison.

JOACHIM MURAT & CAROLINE BONAPARTE, KING & QUEEN OF NAPLES

1802

When the Marriage Contract was signed Caroline had a dowry of 40,000 francs and 12,000 francs-worth of jewels.

Caroline, youngest sister of Napoleon, beautiful and spoilt, met one of his Generals, Joachim Murat early in 1797 when she was being fêted by Italian society.

She fell madly in love with his curly black hair, his panache and reputation for bravery. Murat, who was an innkeeper's son, paid little attention to her as he had at that time at least two mistresses, and Caroline returned to school in France.

She met him again sixteen months later, after he had been severely wounded during the Egyptian War. This time he noticed her fresh beauty, but Caroline again returned to school while Murat aided Napoleon in his bid to oust the Directoire.

After midnight on the night of the coup, Murat sent four grenadiers to inform Caroline that her brother was safe and had been appointed First Consul.

Caroline and Murat then asked Napoleon for permission to marry.

'I don't like these love matches,' Napoleon replied. But after two months of tears and recriminations he surrendered. Murat, writing to his brother André before the wedding, said:

'Tomorrow I shall be the happiest of men, tomorrow I shall possess the most lovable of women.'

Napoleon made Murat King of Naples in 1808.

HRH Princess Charlotte of Great Britain
& HH Prince Leopold of Saxe-Coburg

1816

Princess Charlotte. Impulsive, gauche, hoydenish but warm-hearted.

Prince Leopold. Handsome, controlled, intelligent, ambitious.

Princess Charlotte, only child of George IV, was bright, witty and warm-hearted with large light-blue eyes. As she was heir to the throne there were many suggestions as to whom she should marry. She momentarily thought herself in love with the Crown Prince of Prussia although she was slightly attached to blond, good-looking Prince Leopold of Saxe-Coburg.

Shortly before Christmas 1815 Charlotte had an affectionate meeting with the Prince and later that day she wrote to her father: 'I no longer hesitate in

Prince Leopold and Princess Charlotte at the theatre. The Prince a solemn, dutiful young man of 26 patiently tamed Charlotte's wilder manners.

declaring my partiality in favour of the Prince of Coburg.'

They were married the following year and Charlotte was lovingly contented with her husband.

'We live a very quiet and retired life here,' she wrote from Claremont House in Surrey, 'but a very, *very* happy one.'

For the first time in her life she took criticism without resentment. '*Doucement, ma chérie, doucement*', Leopold would say, and she would try to please him.

When she died in childbirth in 1817, through the inefficiency of her doctors, Leopold was overwhelmed with grief.

HCM Maria Cristina, Queen Regent of Spain & Don Augustin Fernando Muñoz y Sanchez

1833

The Queen Regent fell in love at first sight.

The Queen Regent of Spain was twenty-six when her husband, King Fernando VIII, whom she had nursed devotedly, died in 1833. Very attractive, when she smiled 'every man's heart was at her feet'.

A Bourbon, she had a passionate nature which had been suppressed while she was the fourth wife of an ill old man. She met Fernando Muñoz, a Corporal in the Guards, during an afternoon drive.

The Queen's nose began to bleed and, having used up her own handkerchieves and those of her ladies-in-waiting, they borrowed one from their escort. When the Queen returned it to the Corporal she saw he was a dark, muscular, noble, if somewhat sensual-looking man. With flamboyant chivalry he raised the blood-stained handkerchief to his lips.

For months the Corporal haunted the ardent young Queen's dreams until, again in a coach, she was travelling across the snow-covered Guadarrama mountains escorted by two officers and Corporal Muñoz. They skidded, there was an

The Queen Regent with her troops.

accident and again the Corporal offered his handkerchief.

Later the Queen suggested a walk with one
officer and the Corporal. Some distance from the
house she sent the officer back for an umbrella.

Alone with the man she loved, the Queen told
him of her feelings. That a Queen should take a
lover was nothing new, but this Queen proposed
marriage. Muñoz, the son of simple people who
kept a tobacco shop, fell on his knees and burst
into tears.

After three months of widowhood, the Queen
was married secretly and was wildly, ecstatically
happy. Muñoz moved into the Palace as Groom of
the Bedchamber, and unlike other Royal favour-
ites was not ambitious for power or title. The
Queen had four children by him and had the
greatest difficulties in keeping her pregnancies
hidden.

Muñoz was created Duke de Riansares, deco-
rated with the Order of the Golden Fleece and
raised to the rank of a Grandee of the First Order.

*The Queen wearing the amazing jewels belonging to the
Crown.*

43

HH Prince Ferdinand of Saxe-Coburg
& HRH Dona Maria da Gloria

1836

Only after insurrection, rebellions and terrible hazards did Ferdinand manage to follow his true interest, the encouragement of Arts and the Sciences.

Maria da Gloria was the daughter of Dom Pedro, Emperor of Brazil, son of King João VI of Portugal. In 1826 her father renounced the crown of Portugal in favour of his six-year-old daughter, Maria da Gloria, on condition she would one day marry her uncle – Dom Miguel, sixteen years her senior.

No sooner had Dom Miguel, a handsome and dashing Prince, become Regent than he usurped his niece's throne.

Maria da Gloria who was brought up in England with Queen Victoria, was declared of age when she was fifteen and was recognized as Queen of Portugal.

In 1836 Prince Ferdinand of Saxe-Coburg, a first cousin of Albert who was to marry the Queen Victoria, arrived in Lisbon. He was nineteen, tall, clean-shaven with fair hair and blue eyes. Maria fell in love with him and he was 'much pleased' with his pretty, plump bride.

Maria was a more docile wife than Queen Victoria and bore her adored husband eleven children.

Queluz Royal Palace.

45

HM QUEEN VICTORIA OF GREAT BRITAIN
& HH PRINCE ALBERT OF SAXE-COBURG AND GOTHA
1840

When Victoria came to the throne in 1837, her youth, her sweetness and her desire to 'be good' brought tears to the eyes of her elderly Statesmen.

When she was nineteen, she was crowned and the next step had to be her marriage. She did not really want to think about it, but it seemed the only way of ridding herself of her mother.

Prince Albert of Saxe-Coburg and Gotha was recommended to her, but she replied, she might well like him 'as a friend and as a *cousin* and as a *brother* but nothing *more*'.

'I only felt so happy,' Queen Victoria said of her wedding.

But when she stood on the top of the stairs at Windsor Castle to greet him on his arrival in England in October 1839, she was immediately overwhelmed at the sight of him. He was *'beautiful'*, *'very fascinating'*. He set her heart 'quite going'.

When she asked Prince Albert to marry her in the Blue Closet he took her hands in his and covered them with kisses.

the Empress Eugénie in her bridal dress.
drawing taken from life by E.T. Parris, at the marriage.
of Napn III, Emper of the French) at the ceremonial
wedded at Nôtre Dame, Paris, Sunday Jany 30th 1853

An original
to Chs Louis N

Finally the Emperor, wildly in love, after battling with the almost insuperable task of persuading his Ministers to accept Eugénie, sent a formal request for her hand to her mother.

In January 1853 they were married. Queen Victoria wrote: 'The future bride is beautiful, clever, very *coquette*, passionate and wild.'

On Sunday, the day after the civil ceremony, the Empress joined her husband in the gilded coach which had carried Napoleon I and Josephine to their coronation at Notre-Dame in 1804! Fantastic though the pageantry was, Eugénie stole the day.

For a few months Napoleon and Eugénie were very much in love. An official entering a room at the Tuileries Palace was surprised to see her sitting on his knee.

If they wanted to say private things to each other when other people were there, they spoke English. But Napoleon's frequent desires were uncontrollable. He craved new eyes, new shapes, new sexual experiences.

'I need my little amusements but I always return to her with pleasure,' he told his cousin.

But Eugénie was not prepared to play sweet music on a second string.

HI & RH Franz Joseph, Emperor of Austria, & Elisabeth, Duchess in Bavaria

1854

The most beautiful woman of all time, Elisabeth, Empress of Austria, was to many men a dream come true, but she suffered agonizingly.

The most beautiful Queen of all time, Elisabeth, daughter of Maximilian, Duke in Bavaria, lived a wild, free life with her very Bohemian father.

Her mother, Duchess Ludovika, decided that her eldest daughter Hélène should marry the Emperor, and he was invited to dinner when they were staying at the Austrian Spa Ischl.

Elisabeth, being only sixteen, was to stay in the schoolroom, but at the last moment it was found

The Emperor Franz Joseph.

that there would be thirteen sitting down at the dinner-table.

Dressed in her best gown, she was hurriedly sent downstairs to make the fourteenth person. She was enchantingly lovely and graceful. The handsome young Emperor took one look at Elisabeth and fell madly in love.

When Elisabeth arrived by ship in Vienna on 22 April 1854 to be married, the Emperor, not able to wait for the gangway to be let down, jumped aboard and kissed her passionately, to the wild acclaim of thousands of his delighted and happy subjects.

But the depressing protocol of the Hapsburg

Elisabeth was only really happy and free when she was riding and training her beloved horses.

Palace and the hostility of her mother-in-law, the formidable Archduchess Sophie, ruined the happiness of the young couple.

The finest horsewoman the world had ever known, Elisabeth only felt free when she was hunting in England or riding wildly across the Steppes of her beloved Hungary, the country that made her its Queen.

Yet Franz Joseph always loved her, and when in 1898 an assassin plunged a knife into her breast, he was heartbroken.

SHEIKH ABDUL MEDJUEL EL MEZRAB
& MISS JANE DIGBY
1856

A great romantic, the greatest beauty of her day, irresistible, fascinating, reckless, with 'blue eyes which could move a saint', Jane Digby's love affairs read like a naughty Almanach de Gotha.

Her husband, Lord Ellenborough, a pompous bore, neglected her. Pregnant, she bolted with her lover Prince Felix Schwarzenberg to Paris. She moved to Munich and this time her lover was a

She craved love, adventure, the joy of living and found it all.

King. Ludwig I was a worshipper of beauty and besotted by beautiful women.

Jane married Baron Carl-Theodore von Venningen, young, handsome and rich. Again it was boring and Count Spyridon Theotoky appeared.

*Blue-blooded,
well-educated, speaking
several languages, with
glittering impenetrable black
eyes, Medjuel captured
Jane's roving romantic
heart.*

There was a duel. Theotoky was wounded. They were married. The Count was appointed Aide-de-Camp to King Otto of Greece, who became Jane's lover, provoking scandal and recriminations from Otto's Queen. Jane lived with the Chief of the Pallikares, a bandit, in the mountains, until he fancied her maid.

While negotiating for a camel caravan to take her across the desert, she met Sheikh Abdul Medjuel el Mezrab – Royal, well-educated, speaking several languages, with glittering impenetrable black eyes. Jane had met her fourth and last husband, the great love of her life.

Jane was loved and accepted by the Mezrab tribe as their Queen. She lived in a tent, hunted with Medjuel; and waited on him. For twenty-five years Jane's marriage to Medjuel was wildly, ecstatically passionate.

HM KING GEORGE I OF GREECE
& HIH GRAND DUCHESS OLGA OF RUSSIA
1867

The King and Queen of Greece very much older.

Prince William of Glücksburg was elected to the throne of Greece as King George I in July 1863. He was only seventeen and 'boyish in many ways, with a flow of spirits which made it difficult sometimes for his daily companions to maintain the respectful reserve and gravity due to his station'.

He took his position very seriously and confided in one of his companions that he was determined to be married as soon as it was possible.

Five years later he had an invitation from the Tsar of Russia to seek a wife. The most suitable was the Grand Duchess Vera, daughter of the Tsar's youngest brother, Grand Duke Constantine.

The King arrived at the Grand Duke's Palace in Pavlovsk and happened to look up in the hall. He saw looking down at him a very shy, fair-haired, lovely young girl. It was the Grand Duke's younger daughter Olga, and it was love at first sight for both of them.

They were married at the Winter Palace in St Petersburg on 27 October 1868. When they left for Greece the newly-wed Queen of the Hellenes, who was not yet sixteen, took her dolls with her.

Grand Duchess Olga at sixteen when the King, aged twenty-two, fell in love with her. Monarchy is obviously ageing!

HRH Crown Prince Frederick of Denmark
& HRH Princess Louise of Sweden and Norway

1869

The Queen of Denmark.

HRH Prince Frederick. Very handsome men often dislike competition and wish for no rivals where their wives are concerned.

Known in his childhood as 'Freddie with the pretty face' it was expected that Crown Prince Frederick of Denmark would make a brilliant marriage. Affable, assured, elegant, charming, cheerful, the Prince at twenty-five was a very eligible Royal bachelor.

To everyone's astonishment he became engaged in 1868 to the seventeen-year-old Princess Louise, only child of the King of Sweden. She had romantic connections with Napoleon Bonaparte and her second name was Josephine, after the Empress, her great-great-grandmother.

She was, however, plain, shy, pious and frumpish – yet Freddie loved her, and they were very happy. They had seven children.

PRINCE SI AHMED & AURÉLIE PICCARD
1871

Aurélie banishes the wives and concubines to a place two days' journey from her new home. The infatuated Si Ahmed agrees.

Prince Si Ahmed, a young Arab ruler from Southern Algeria, was visiting Bordeaux. A very romantic and impressive figure, he wore a dark burnous over another white one, in the belt of which there was a jewelled dagger, and boots of crimson leather. His face was framed by a dark beard.

Prince Si Ahmed was of the noblest Shareefan blood. His followers prostrated themselves before him but in Ain Mahdi there were scorpions, bats, venomous snakes and deadly black spiders.

Surrounded by an entourage of guards, black slaves and courtiers, he saw a beautiful girl feeding a large number of carrier pigeons.

Aurélie Piccard, a little provincial as her father was a poor soldier, had gone out to work at fifteen, apprenticed to a milliner. She became housekeeper to Madame Steenacker, one of her clients whose husband became Directeur Général des Postes at Bordeaux.

At first the Prince and Aurélie had difficulty in communicating, but the more often they met the more madly the Prince fell in love.

He called in Madame Steenacker and asked what he should pay her for Aurélie.

'Aurélie is not for sale,' Madame replied, 'but she could be married.'

'So be it!' the Prince said. 'I will marry her at once.'

Everything was arranged but the French Governor General refused to sanction a Franco-Arab union. Aurélie wept, the Prince pleaded.

Cardinal Lavigérie, Archbishop of Algiers, who was just starting his great missionary work in North Africa intervened. The thwarted lovers intrigued him. He married them in 1871 in a simple Catholic marriage but the Arab festivities lasted for a week with fireworks, music and the Ouled Nail dancers.

A great cortège carried Aurélie on a white Arab mare, saddled in velvet with coral and silver trappings, to Ain Mahdi. The journey took a month and Aurélie, falling more and more in love with her handsome husband, was rapturously happy.

Awaiting her arrival were her mother-in-law, fourteen sisters-in-law, Si Ahmed's wives and concubines, all united in their intention to destroy her.

As if divinely inspired, Aurélie took control of the harem and the *Zaouia*. The wives and concubines were banished, soon her husband's family adored her.

As Lallah Yamma, *la Princesse des Sables*, Aurélie became an invincible power in the Sahara and all over Algeria. Si Ahmed became the mighty Shareif but he never took another wife. Aurélie held him captive by her love.

HCM King Alfonso XII of Spain
& Dona Maria de Las Mercedes

1878

King Alfonso XII, with an olive skin and dark hair, was extremely charming. He also had the Bourbon passions and his love for his wife, the beautiful Mercedes, made their marriage one of the most popular in Spanish history.

Alfonso was only nineteen when he announced he intended to marry Mercedes, the sixteen-year-old daughter of the Duke de Montpensier. They had been in love for two years.

Ex-Queen Isobel was 'outraged'. She had already decided that her son should marry the Pretender's eldest daughter Blanca, who was only ten at the time.

Alfonso had however said: 'I will never marry against my will!'

Mercedes was beautiful, delicate and distinguished, with 'large dark eyes, shadowed by sweeping lashes, her hair was the true Andalusian black'.

The engagement was celebrated by a great ball in December 1877. A month later Alfonso and Mercedes were married, with great pomp, in the Church of the Atocha. The Spaniards gave themselves over to an orgy of rejoicing at the wedding – flags, music, dancing, Royal bull fights with nobles as *toreros*.

'My brother and his wife are idyllically happy in their married life,' said Eulalia, 'and their happiness was reflected in everyone around them.'

An Englishman described Alfonso as 'light, gay, insouciant, loyal – the very picture of Prince Charming', whispering into the ear of his lovely Queen.

Yet five months after their marriage Mercedes died of gastric fever. They dressed her in the black and white habit of a nun.

Alfonso's grief was heart-breaking: he never really recovered, the young and happy part of him was gone.

Tsar Alexander II
& Princess Catherine Dolgornky

1880

When Alexander II first saw Catherine she was twelve years old and he was a tired, lonely, disillusioned but sensual man of forty-two.

He visited her father's estate while on manoeuvres. She was riding her pony who would not jump and the Tsar, whom she did not recognize, teased her. Neither of them ever forgot their first meeting.

In 1865, when the Dolgornkys were in St Petersburg, the Tsar began to court Catherine with bonbons and flowers. By now she was slim with large dark eyes, bright chestnut hair and the skin and animation which go with perfect health.

On 13 July 1866 at an Imperial pavilion in the park of the Winter Palace Catherine became the Tsar's mistress.

Every day he managed to snatch an hour or two with Catherine. He became her slave, her adorer, 'his life . . . his idol . . . for ever'.

Their first child was born secretly in 1872 in the Tsar's study. Three more children were born in the following years.

On 5 June 1880 the unhappy Tsarina died. Forty days later the Tsar married his adored Catherine

with only two witnesses present. She was created Her Serene Highness the Princess Yurievsky, her children taking the same name.

The Tsar's passion was now unbridled; he smothered her in jewels, settled a huge fortune and properties in Russia and abroad on her.

Eight months after the wedding on Sunday 13 March 1881 the Tsar's carriage was shattered by terrorists' bombs. 'To the Palace – to die,' he muttered.

They laid him on the sofa where he had so often kissed Catherine.

When she was fetched the Princess was wearing only a fine negligée. With a heart-rending scream she fell across the body of her husband.

'Sasha! Sasha!' she cried, but he could not hear her. His blood soaked her ribbons and laces. In an hour he was dead.

Nothing clouded the love the Tsar had for his 'wife before God', they 'plunge into ecstasy on the verge of madness'.

Below. The Tsar's drawing, dated 1869, of his 'adorable IMP'.

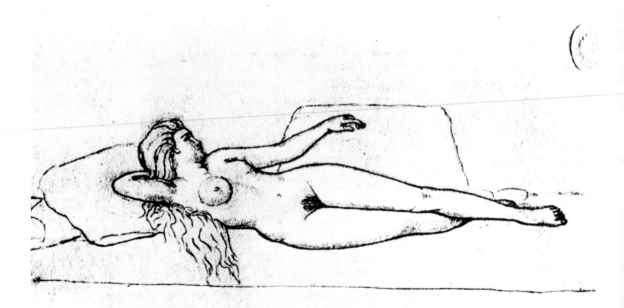

HM King Alexander i of Bulgaria
& Miss Louise Loisinger
1889

Mlle Loisinger as she appeared in the Opera Faust and Marguerite.

Prince Alexander of Bulgaria, handsome, charming, brave and headstrong.

King Alexander, clever and attractive, known in the family as Sandio, was the son of Prince Alexander of Hesse and his morganatic wife who became Princess of Battenberg. He was a particular favourite of Queen Victoria and at the age of twenty-two was chosen to rule Bulgaria, one of the new Balkan States created by the Congress of Berlin in 1878.

Unfortunately although very brave he was no diplomat and his relations with the Tsar went from bad to worse. In 1886 the Russians organized a Military conspiracy in Sofia, forcing King Alexander to sign his Abdication under fear of death.

They then handcuffed him and took him off to Russia. Queen Victoria never forgave 'these Russian fiends' and the Bulgarians wept in the streets.

He fell, however, madly in love with beautiful, young, golden-voiced Louise Loisinger, an opera star of the Darmstadt Court Theatre. Alexander renounced his rank and titles to marry her in 1889.

His cousin Grand Duke Louis IV of Hesse gave him the non-Royal title of Count Hartenau. Wearing the grand crosses of thirty-six different orders, which Kings and Emperors had given him in his days of glory, he entered the Austrian Army as a Lieutenant Colonel.

HSH PRINCE ALBERT I OF MONACO
& THE DUCHESSE DE RICHELIEU
1892

Princess Alice, formerly Duchesse de Richelieu.

Prince Albert of Monaco and his toy Palace.

Prince Albert's first marriage to Lady Mary Douglas Hamilton, daughter of the eleventh Duke of Hamilton, was a failure from the start. He and the bride were forced into it by their parents and Napoleon III.

The marriage was annulled by the Vatican and in 1892 the Prince married Alice Heine, widow of the Duc de Richelieu. She was the first American to marry a reigning European Sovereign. She was beautiful, accomplished and a great patron of the arts. She made Monaco the centre for opera, ballet and the theatre.

Alas, their happiness only lasted for ten years.

HRH Prince George, Duke of York
& HH Princess May of Teck

1893

'I saw in you the person I was capable of loving most deeply, if you only returned that love . . . I have tried to understand you and know you, and with the happy result that I know now that I do love you, darling girl, with all my heart, and am simply devoted to you, I adore you, sweet May, I can't say more than this.'

Prince George, quiet, dependable, shy, enjoyed stamp collecting and billiards.
Princess May, reserved, careful, shy, well-educated, excellent memory, liked collecting antiques.

George, Duke of York was married on 6 July 1893 to Princess May of Teck, and he wrote this letter some months after their wedding.

The Princess was acutely shy and the Duke, while highly emotional, found it hard to express what he felt. They wrote passionate love letters to each other but found it difficult to break through their traditional Victorian reserve when they were face to face.

Princess May (publicly she was called Mary after she married) replied to one of her husband's letters: 'What a pity it is that you cannot *tell* me

The Marriage in the Chapel Royal, St James's Palace. Queen Victoria a diminutive figure, Princess Alexandra wistful and beautiful, and the Tsarevitch Nicholas unbelievably like the bridegroom.

HRH Crown Princess Louise of Saxony
& Signor Enrico Toselli
1907

The Princess married to get away from home, but her husband never loved her so she tried to console herself by collecting insects.

Crown Princess Louise, a rebellious Hapsburg Archduchess of Tuscany, hated her father-in-law King Johann I. He loathed her for laughing at Court etiquette and bicycling in knickerbockers. He was sure the hereditary madness of the Hapsburgs would appear if she ever became Queen, and arranged to lock her away in a private lunatic asylum.

The Princess wisely ran away and, after her marriage to her good-natured husband Friedrich (who was to be the last King of Saxony) was annulled, she married an Italian composer and pianist, Enrico Toselli, by whom she had two children.

The Princess was forbidden to return to, or communicate with, the children of her first marriage. Incognito, she travelled to Dresden to see them but was bundled back on the train by the Chief of Police amidst tears from the loyal people, who filled her carriage with flowers.

HRH Prince Ernst August of Hanover
& HRH Princess Viktoria Luise of Prussia

1913

The Bride and Bridegroom.

'For me it was love at first sight. Suddenly I was all fire and flame,' Princess Viktoria Luise said the first time she met Prince Ernst August, wearing his blue Bavarian uniform of the Heavy Cavalry Regiment.

Until he came to tea, while her family was in Potsdam, she had no idea that he existed.

It was some time before she learnt that the Prince had the same feelings about her, but there were many difficulties, especially as the Prince's parents loathed the new German Reich and its Emperors.

Then, in January 1913, a telegram told the anxious couple that these were overcome and their happiness could not be kept secret.

The wedding, which took place in Berlin in 1913, was one of the last opulent Royal occasions of old Europe.

The celebrations ended with the *Fackeltanz*, or torch dance – a dance only performed at German Royal weddings, and in which no one below the rank of Royal Highness was allowed to take part.

Prince Ernst August's Court was brilliant, well-organized and extremely hospitable although he and the Princess had simple tastes. He found elaborate Court ceremonial humbug, and to people who began with traditional form of 'Allow me to throw myself at Your Majesty's feet,' he would retort: 'Rubbish, if you did, you would split your trousers.'

His happiness with his wife undoubtedly gave him strength. But he was shy of being demonstrative in public. As he had said to her when they were engaged:

'I don't like people to be there and stare, for they are all killjoys.'

HH Princess Indira of Baroda
& HH The Maharaja of Cooch Behar

1913

'Wherever she went, hearts were shattered like egg-shells.'

This was written of a raving beauty, the Princess Indira, only daughter of the progressively minded, saintly Maharaja Sayaji Rao of Baroda. The trouble was that the Princess's own heart remained unmoved. By the time she was sixteen, and not affianced, it meant in the Hindu tradition that she was on the shelf. The Princes in India left her cold, so her parents took her in 1911 to London for the Coronation of King George V.

Here Indira met Sir Madhav Rao Sindia Maharajah of Gwalior, a bustling tiger-hunter. Worn down at last, she agreed to become his second wife. The engagement was announced when Indira fell in love!

Handsome, poetic, eight years older than she, Jitendra was the second son of the Maharaja of Cooch Behar, a controversial family of a different faith to the Barodas.

A very untraditional Indian wedding, but they had fought and won and were together at last.

Indira secretly sent a letter to her fiancé telling him their marriage was off, and in the row that followed she and Jitendra were forbidden to see each other.

A few stolen meetings, notes, tears – but nothing more, and after two years the lovers were desperate. They planned an elopement, it was discovered and Indira was guarded everywhere she went, while her parents would not speak to her.

The Barodas went to St Moritz. Jitendra booked into another hotel, planning to elope again when he learnt that his brother, after two years on the throne, was dying in England.

The Barodas gave in, and Indira married her love in a Register Office and with Brahmo rites in the Buckingham Palace Hotel.

HM KING ALEXANDER I OF GREECE
& ASPASIA MANOS

1919

Aspasia Manos was the daughter of an Aide-de-Camp to King Constantine, who had abdicated. She was exquisitely beautiful, with a profile like one of the nymphs in a classical Greek frieze come to life.

King Alexander I, the second son of King Constantine, had known her since they were children together.

One night in November 1919, a priest in the poorer quarter of Athens was woken by a loud knocking on his door. He went downstairs and was told he was needed urgently, then driven to a private house.

King Alexander was good-looking, attractive and determined when he wanted his own way. The happiness he found with his wife was some compensation for a life of disappointment and humiliation.

As she fought to marry the man she loved, so she fought for her daughter, Princess Alexandra, when they had to flee to England during the last war.

As soon as he arrived King Alexander, an attractive young man, and Aspasia entered and asked the priest to marry them.

There was consternation when the secret was disclosed.

The King had married without the consent of his father, or the Head of the Church. What was more, the populace was furious, being determined not to have a commoner on the throne.

Finally it was decided Madame Manos, as she was called, should have no rank or privilege, but her daughter should be given the title of HRH Princess Alexandra of Greece.

Despite such difficulties, while King Alexander was alive they were very happy, but he died in 1920 from blood poisoning following a monkey bite.

HRH Prince Albert, Duke of York, & The Lady Elizabeth Bowes-Lyon

1923

The Duke and Duchess of York.

In the woods of St Paul's Walden Bury in Hertfordshire, HRH Prince Albert, Duke of York, second son of George V, begged Lady Elizabeth Bowes-Lyon to marry him. They had met at a dance three years earlier, and although the Duke was very shy, and found it hard to express his feelings, he realized later he had fallen in love.

It was not surprising. As someone wrote, 'her radiant vitality, and a blending of gaiety, kindness and sincerity made her irresistible to men'.

Lady Elizabeth Bowes-Lyon also had, beneath her soft, gentle manner, a good sense of humour and an enjoyment of the ridiculous.

When the Duke told his father whom he wanted to marry, George V merely replied: 'You will be lucky if she accepts you.'

The Duke was unlucky, and Lady Elizabeth did refuse him, but they continued to meet. Again she refused him, but there was still hope because the Duke was invited to Glamis, the great Castle of the Strathmore family in Scotland.

Afterwards, Lady Strathmore wrote of her daughter:

'I think Elizabeth was torn between her longing to make Bertie happy and her reluctance to take on the big responsibilities which the marriage must bring.'

But in the New Year Bertie sent a telegram to his parents at Sandringham in the code they had arranged. It said simply, 'ALL RIGHT BERTIE.'

Their great happiness together, the support the Duchess of York gave her husband when on the abdication of Edward VIII he became King George VI, the way she helped him over his speaking difficulties, and how she conquered Britain with her smile is all part of our history.

Elizabeth the Queen Mother is unique. There is no Queen or commoner like her.

The marriage service at Westminster Abbey in the presence of the King, Queen, Prince of Wales, Queen Alexandra and Princess Mary.

Leaving home for a very different life.

With an old cannon at historic Glamis Castle.

On a Royal Tour in 1927. The Duke and Duchess of York take a trip down Brisbane River on a visit to the Anzee Hostel. The Duke had loved his life in the Navy and was always happy afloat.

The Duchess of York launches a New Cruiser, HMS York, in Palmer's Yard, Barrow on Tyne.

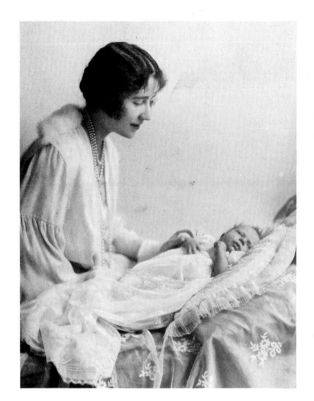

The Duchess with Princess Elizabeth, who was born at 2.40 am on 21 April 1926 by a caesarean section at her grandparents' house in Bruton Street.

King George VI and Queen Elizabeth with their two daughters, Elizabeth and Margaret Rose, at Royal Lodge, Windsor.

King George VI and Queen Elizabeth wearing their State Robes in the Throne Room at Buckingham Palace in 1948.

HRH PRINCE PAUL OF YUGOSLAVIA
& HRH PRINCESS OLGA OF GREECE

1923

The wedding group after the ceremony in Belgrade.

'Why the hell should Olga marry him if she doesn't love him?', eleven-year-old Marina asked.

Olga, her elder sister and the eldest daughter of Prince Nicholas of Greece, had become engaged to Crown Prince Frederick of Denmark. But suddenly they quarrelled and the engagement was broken off.

There was consternation in the family and everyone discussed how the young couple could be forced to 'make it up'. But Marina's question was unanswerable, and the Prince returned home to Denmark.

A little later in 1923, Olga met Prince Paul of Yugoslavia at a ball in England. Although he stared at her for most of the evening they were not introduced. When he returned to his flat he could not sleep. It was not until 10 July that Paul succeeded in meeting Olga. On Friday 13 he danced with her at a ball, and ten days later they were together at another ball at Hurlingham.

By now Paul was deeply and hopelessly in love and Olga noted in her diary: 'I sat out the whole of the evening with Paul and didn't feel a bit bored.'

He took Olga to a cinema, as he seemed nervous she asked: 'Have you found what you want?' He replied fervently, 'Yes, at last.'

It was a deep, lasting love for both of them. He was clever, sensitive and artistic. She was philosophical, practical and a very merry person.

After they were married Princess Olga wrote, 'Our happiness, mine at least, increases daily and time seems to fly.'

Their marriage was ideally happy.

After the wedding they went to Venice.

The portrait of Olga was by her sister Marina, the Duchess of Kent.

Prince Paul and Princess Olga in the Court-coach, behind them the Commander of the Croatian Peasant Guard.

HRH Prince George, Duke of Kent, & HRH Princess Marina of Greece

1934

Princess Marina's gown was of shining silver lamé. The Prince of Wales was best man and Princess Elizabeth was a bridesmaid.

Dashing, high-spirited Prince George was not afraid of anyone or anything. He was the only one of the Royal children who was not frightened when their father King George V erupted into one of his rages.

He adored speed, dancing, flying and pretty women. When he saw the uniquely beautiful Princess Marina of Greece, he fell head-over-heels in love.

Marina and her three sisters had grown up in an informal atmosphere. Their father, Prince Nicholas, was an artist of some exceptional talent, and Marina studied art in Paris as an ordinary student, travelling on the Metro alone. She had very little money.

She, too, fell in love as soon as she met Prince George, they became engaged in Bohiny when they were both staying with Prince Paul of Yugoslavia, who had married her elder sister Olga.

When on 28 August 1934 the engagement was announced, Princess Marina was so unknown in England that Fleet Street had no photographs of her; later, because she was so beautiful, no Royal was more photographed.

For eight years the Duke and Duchess of Kent were ecstatically happy together and they had three children.

With King George, Queen Mary, Prince and Princess Nicholas of Greece.

On 25 August 1942 the Duke, who was in the RAF, set off in a Sunderland flying boat on a secret mission to Ireland. Owing to bad weather the plane was forced to fly low and crashed into the last mountain in Scotland. The Duke was killed instantly.

On the balcony at Buckingham Palace.

HM KING EDWARD VIII
& MRS WALLIS SIMPSON

1937

'Prince Charming', the most attractive, charming, eligible bachelor in the world, Edward, Prince of Wales, had been pursued by beautiful women since he left Dartmouth Naval Training College. Then at nearly forty he met the love of his life.

His passion for an American woman who had divorced one husband and was married to another was to become the most controversial and most explosive love-story in British history.

Born in Baltimore, amusing, provocative, immaculate, soignée, Wallis Simpson was not beautiful, but the Prince found her completely irresistible.

By the time he became King he was determined to marry her, even if it meant giving up his throne

As Edward walked behind his father's coffin the sapphire and diamond Maltese Cross on top of the Imperial Crown broke off and rolled on the ground. A Sergeant-Major retrieved it as the King exclaimed: 'Christ! What's going to happen next?'

The Duke and Duchess in Paris in 1937. Her jewellery was always fabulous, her clothes ahead of the latest fashion.

Poignant nose, blue eyes, fair skin, gold hair, a Dream Prince.

and an Empire covering a quarter of the Earth's surface.

'It appears that the King is Mrs Simpson's absolute slave and will go nowhere when she is not invited,' wrote one diarist at the time.

The drama which was enacted over Mrs Simpson's divorce, the pressure from the newspapers, her flight to France, hotly pursued by the press, the tragic abdication and the marriage of the Duke of Windsor to the Duchess with no Royal rank is all in the history books.

Perhaps the Prime Minister's wife, Mrs Baldwin, summed it all up in one sentence: 'God grant him peace and happiness but never an understanding of what he has lost.'

HH THE MAHARAJA OF JAIPUR
& HH PRINCESS AYESHA OF COOCH BEHAR
1940

Ayesha, born in 1919, one of the most beautiful women in the world, was the daughter of the Maharaja of Cooch Behar.

Her brother was crowned Maharaja at the age of seven, and a year later was sent to a 'prep' school in England, leaving behind his Royal palace with five hundred servants.

The whole family went with him. Their mother hunted with the Quorn and the Cottesmore.

Ayesha and her sisters went to school in England, and she did not return to India until she was twelve.

In 1931 she met the Maharaja of Jaipur, a very good-looking young man who as India's leading polo player was a hero. The next year Jai, as he was always called, went to Calcutta to win the Polo Championship and took Ayesha – still only a child – out to dinner.

When Ayesha was thirteen Jai was being married to his second wife. A year later she realized she was hopelessly in love with him.

Elephants lift their trunks and bellow a salute.

Two years later he told her that long ago he had told her mother he wanted to marry her when she was grown up, but the Maharani had laughed at the idea.

Below. Part of Marriage Ceremony.

The fabulous pink Palaces of Jaipur.

Somehow they managed to meet secretly. They gave each other gold rings with their names engraved on the inside.

Ayesha's mother now knew of their love for each other, but disapproved of her daughter becoming a third wife. Finally she said they must wait two years.

War, however, brought things to a head, and Jai persuaded Ayesha they could wait no longer, so in 1940 they were finally engaged.

With two hundred saris and a procession of forty elephants, Ayesha was married with all the ceremonial of a Rajputan bride. She lived in the exquisite pink city of Jaipur where later she and Jai were to entertain the Queen of England and Prince Philip.

She was the first Maharani to be elected as a Member of Parliament and she travelled thousands of miles electioneering, encouraged and helped by Jai. She won by 175,000 votes over her opponent.

The most beautiful married couple in the world and so very, very much in love.

HRH PRINCESS ELIZABETH
& LIEUTENANT PHILIP MOUNTBATTEN
1947

Princess Elizabeth, steadfast, intuitive, an amazingly retentive memory, brilliantly clever.

Prince Philip. Handsome, dashing, outspoken, determined and very attractive.

Lieutenant Philip Mountbatten, RN was a very handsome, attractive and charming young man. It was not surprising that Princess Elizabeth fell in love with him, and he with her.

Coming back on HMS Vanguard from South Africa where she had been with her parents, Princess Elizabeth danced a little jig with joy on deck when she saw the English coastline, wildly happy that their engagement would soon be announced.

During the war the Princess had been a Second Subaltern in the ATS but she was still very young and inexperienced. When Philip Mountbatten first fell in love with her he was twenty-two and

she was seventeen. They had to wait four years!

They were married on 20 November 1947 and looked radiantly happy. They spent their honeymoon at Broadlands, the home of Earl Mountbatten of Burma, the bridegroom's uncle, whose friendship, counsel and advice was to mean a great deal in the years to come.

Prince Philip, Duke of Edinburgh is five years older than the Queen, and he has been a rock of strength in her very arduous and exacting life. His sense of humour has also smoothed a path which is often thorny despite her brilliant intelligence and astounding knowledge of world affairs.

On the Balcony at
Buckingham Palace after
their wedding. The
Princess's gown is now in
the London Museum. The
Best Man was the Marquis
of Milford Haven. Their
presents included a loincloth
woven by Mahatma Gandhi
himself.

The Queen at this ceremony was described as 'quite perfect' and Sir Winston Churchill saw her as 'the young and gleaming champion' of a wise and kindly way of life. Prince Philip was 'like a Mediaeval Knight'.

HM King Carol II of Roumania
& Madame Elena Lupescu
1947

King Carol had an emotional hunger for love and understanding. Tall, handsome and extremely intelligent, he was expected to be a popular and successful monarch.

Unfortunately he was fatally weak where women were concerned. He made a runaway marriage in 1918 which was annulled, he fell in love with the beautiful Princess Helen of Greece and married her. But in 1925 he met *une femme fatale*.

Elena Lupescu forced Carol to renounce his rights to the throne. When his father died, the government invited him to return to Roumania as King. Elena followed him there although he had promised she would stay away. His downfall came when Elena's influence caused him to be rude to his mother and unkind to his wife.

When in 1940 Hitler engineered his deposition and exile, Carol had no friends left.

Elena never lost her passionate allure for him. In exile in Portugal they were married in a Civil Ceremony in 1947 and a religious one in 1949.

HSH Prince Rainier iii of Monaco
& Miss Grace Kelly

1956

The wedding of Prince Rainier, ruler of the romantic 467-acre Principality of Monaco, caused the greatest 'ballyhoo' of the century, but the lovely filmstar Grace Kelly has since, with her charm and her intelligence, been a model of Royal dignity.

It was a love-match which has grown and strengthened with the years, and is very different to the turbulent marriages and the turbulent reigns of the Prince's Grimaldi ancestors, who date back to the eleventh century.

There is so much magic about Monaco that it is right that the magical Princess Grace, who grows more beautiful every year, should reign over this fantastic little Kingdom.

HM BAUDOUIN, KING OF THE BELGIANS, & DONA FABIOLA MORA Y ARAGON

1960

King Baudouin had been on the throne for nine years before he fell in love with an attractive Spaniard. They were married in December 1960 but it has been a deep sadness that they have no children.

Before her marriage Queen Fabiola published a children's book called *The Twelve Marvellous Tales*, and the proceeds from the sales go to the National Society for Children. The Queen also has a special secretariat at the Palace to deal with all the enquiries she receives about handicapped children.

Princess Margaret has a flare for design and decor. She would have been a brilliant stage producer and if it had been possible an even more brilliant actress. She has always longed for far-off horizons and like everyone who reaches for the stars she has been bitterly disappointed and disillusioned. But she has the courage to survive.

HRH Princess Margaret
& Antony Armstrong-Jones
1960

Princess Margaret was the fairy-tale bride whom every girl dreamt of being. When she was a child she was called Margaret Rose, which was very appropriate to her tiny figure and the huge expressive eyes dominating her oval face.

Love made her on 6 May 1960 lovelier than she had ever been in her thirty years. She had already suffered deeply through love when she had wanted to marry handsome Group Captain Peter Townsend, the King's RAF Equerry. Because he had been divorced she made a public statement:

'I have been aware that, subject to my renouncing my rights of succession, it might have been possible for me to contract a civil marriage. But mindful of the Church's teaching that Christian marriage is indissoluble, and conscious of my duty to the Commonwealth, I have resolved to put these considerations before any others.'

This picture is so beautiful it might have been taken by Antony Armstrong-Jones himself.

Her courage was very touching and now she had found happiness with Antony Armstrong-Jones the whole country wished her well.

He, a brilliant photographer, had an artistic background. His uncle was the famous theatrical designer Oliver Messell, and his mother, now the Countess of Rosse, was one of the most beautiful of the famous beauties in the 'twenties.

As Princess Margaret and Antony Armstrong-Jones – later to be the Earl of Snowdon – walked down the aisle, love seemed to vibrate from them and fill the Abbey with light.

To the crowds watching it was a fairy story come true, but alas, like fairy gold, it eventually vanished at the touch of human hands.

HRH Prince Edward, Duke of Kent,
& Miss Katharine Worsley
1961

Prince 'Eddie' was the eldest of the Duke and Duchess's three children, and as his sister Princess Alexandra was only fourteen months younger they were very close to each other.

After the Duke of Kent was killed flying, the family was very hard up. The Duchess had only a widow's pension and many of the Duke's private collection of antiques had to be sold.

In 1950 Prince Edward, with his Regiment, the Royal Scots Greys at Catterick Camp in Yorkshire, was invited to dance at Hovingham Hall, owned by Sir William Worsley.

As soon as the Duke saw his host's lovely daughter Katharine he fell in love.

But a whirlwind marriage was not allowed. The two lovers spent the next four years apart, Katharine working in a jewellery store in Vancouver, the Prince abroad with his Regiment.

They were married in 1961 at York Minster. Katharine's dress had a train fifteen feet long. Two thousand guests were entertained at Hovingham Hall before the happy couple boarded a Heron of the Queen's Flight to take them on their honeymoon.

HRH Prince Juan Carlos of Spain & HRH Princess Sofia of Greece

1962

Beneath the handsome exterior of the King lies a self-discipline which enabled him to control himself patiently during the long years when he was groomed as Franco's Successor as the Ruler of Spain. Only now is he putting forward his modern, progressive ideas in a country where the cry 'Death to Liberty' can still be heard.

Queen Sofia also learnt patience when she trained as a nurse, and her compassionate understanding is of inestimable help to the husband she loves. She also adores her children and their home vibrates with love and laughter.

Prince Juan Carlos, the only son of Don Juan, the Count of Barcelona, was sixteen when in 1954 he fell in love with Princess Sofia on the King of Greece's yacht on a cruise in the Mediterranean.

She was only fifteen, and they did not meet again until the Rome Olympics in 1960 when Princess Sofia's brother Constantine won an Olympic gold medal for sailing.

They met again the following year in York at the Duke of Kent's marriage to Katharine Worsley.

They knew then they could not live without each other and Juan Carlos asked King Paul's permission to marry Sofia.

They had two ceremonies at their wedding – one Catholic and one Greek Orthodox.

Juan Carlos was groomed to become General Franco's successor, and his reign was inaugurated in 1975 by a solemn High Mass in Madrid.

Spain had a King again for the first time in forty-four years.

HH Maharaj-Prince Sikkim Palden Thondup Namgyal
& Miss Hope Cooke
1963

The Bride during the Wedding Ceremony in the Buddhist Chapel.

The King and Queen in the beautiful Gardens of the Palace and during their Coronation in Ganglok.

A widower, the Prince met his future wife in the tea lounge of an hotel in Darjeeling in India. Miss Cooke, aged twenty-one, had been in Sikkim to study Oriental languages. Her family ancestry went back to the *Mayflower*. Her uncle, with whom she lived, was in the US Diplomatic Corps and had been Ambassador to the Netherlands, Panama, Iran and Peru.

After their first meeting Hope and the Prince wrote to each other and she told her American friends he was 'a very wise and good man'.

'He proposed to me on the dance floor,' she reported in 1961. 'I said, Yes, Yes, Yes. There was no great design on my part to catch a King. I just fell in love with his sad, sad, sad eyes, and sad smile and beautifully courteous manners.'

Their wedding was spectacular. There were 15,000 guests, while 400 chickens, 100 goats and 200 pigs were needed for the Royal feast.

The Prince wore bright yellow silk and gold brocade; Princess Hopla, Consort of the Deities, wore white, heavily ornamented gold bracelets and a heavy gold belt that held a small dagger.

The Prince became King after his father's death

in 1963. Sikkim is a poor country and Queen Hopla contributed to the Royal finances with her large fortune.

The Palace with its beautiful grounds was a Shangri-La to the Royal couple, and Queen Hopla started writing the history of her new country.

HRH Princess Alexandra of Kent
& The Hon. Angus Ogilvy
1963

Alexandra was the first Royal Princess to go to a boarding school in England. Daughter of the handsome and charming Prince George and the lovely Princess Marina, Duke and Duchess of Kent, it would have been surprising if she, too, had not been beautiful with an irresistible appeal to everyone she met.

The Duke of Kent was killed flying in 1942 and his widow and family were left very badly off. Nevertheless Alexandra was sent to a finishing school in Paris where she became proficient in French, Russian literature and domestic science.

She was only seventeen when she made her first public appearance as a Royal Princess. Later she undertook some of the rigorous overseas tours to Thailand, Borneo, Hong Kong, Japan and Australia, where she was an overwhelming success.

She met Angus Ogilvy, tall, dark, handsome and very clever, at the Beagles Ball at Eton; after that they were frequently together and obviously very much in love.

Angus was a successful businessman, but he came from a famous Scottish family with Royal connections. All the same it was a surprise when the announcement of the engagement was made on 29 November 1962.

They were married on 24 April 1963 and the Princess brought the sunshine into Westminster Abbey in a gown of gold sequins.

Angus Ogilvy refuses to accept a title and does not share his wife's public duties but they are very happy in their private life.

Princess Alexandra is loved wherever she goes because she is so human. 'Was I awful?' she asked when she made her first speech. On her Australian tour she stepped into an open car and sat down on her host's top hat!

HRH Crown Princess Beatrix of the Netherlands & Claus von Amsberg

1966

The Royal Family Wedding Group with the crowds rioting and shouting outside.

'I assure you it is a good thing,' Queen Juliana said on nationwide radio and television when in July 1965 she announced the engagement of her daughter Beatrix to Claus-Georg von Amsberg.

The Dutch people did not think so, Claus had worn the hated uniform of the Nazi Wehrmacht and been a member of the Hitler Youth.

There were marches, rallies, and demonstrations. Crowds shouted: *'Claus raus! Claus raus!'* The Dutch press, who were most pro-Royalty, were deeply disturbed.

Few people knew how hard Queen Juliana had tried to prevent the marriage, even attempting to get Claus, a diplomat, transferred out of Europe.

But Beatrix, who was deeply in love, went on a three-day hunger strike and her mother gave in.

Claus, slim, smiling, and certainly handsome, did not look like a Nazi. He frankly explained at a press conference that he was in love with Beatrix, sorry about his past and fervently wished to be accepted by the Dutch people.

Then Princess Beatrix dropped another bombshell, by announcing she would be married in Amsterdam, a city which had suffered severely from German bombs.

'If I win the hearts of the Amsterdamers,' she declared, 'I will win the hearts of all the Netherlands.'

Princess Beatrix and Claus von Amsberg showed great courage on their Wedding Day. They knew their reception would be hostile and faced it bravely.

A crowd of only 2000 cheered them on the balcony and an effort to raise $350,000 for a present for the bride produced $20,000.

There has never been such a wedding day! An angry march on the Palace, demonstrators fighting with police, tear gas clouding the air, protestors smashing windows and cars destroyed!

More bombs, smoke and stink, and three swastikas were thrown at the golden coach. There were cries for the abolition of the Monarchy.

But love has triumphed! Very happy together, Queen Beatrix and Prince Claus are winning the hearts of the Dutch people and their three sons are irresistibly powerful advocates for their parents.

HRH Princess Margrethe of Denmark
& Count Henri de Laborde de Montpezat

1967

Queen Margrethe became the first Queen regnant of Denmark in six hundred years.

She is very clever, had a remarkable all-round education and is a graduate of five Universities.

She met her husband in 1963 in London. Henri Laborde de Montpezat who is charming, polished and French, was the Third Secretary at the French Embassy. They fell in love and Henri was made Prince Henrik of Denmark on their marriage in 1967.

The Queen, called 'Daisy' by her close friends, has a passion for archaeology, clothes and bridge!

Denmark is one of the oldest Kingdoms in Europe and Queen Margrethe loves ruling over it. 'It is no strain,' she said, 'I enjoy doing it. It is a happy duty.'

HRH Crown Prince Harald of Norway
& Miss Sonja Haraldsen

1968

King Olav of Norway looks like Santa Claus and the whole house, twelve miles from Oslo, vibrates with peals of laughter! His grandchildren Prince Haaken Magnus and Princess Martha Louise adore him and because their parents are so happy they live in a world filled with love.

Crown Prince Harald fell in love with Sonja Haraldsen, an Oslo draper's daughter, when they were both in their teens.

They had to fight fervently for several frustrating years until, in 1968, the marriage was allowed.

The Prince is tall, very good-looking and exceedingly popular. Princess Sonja adores him.

People say proudly that she 'belongs to the people' and will, when the time comes, be 'every inch a Queen!'

HRH PRINCESS ANNE
& CAPTAIN MARK PHILLIPS

1973

An outstanding rider in any century, Princess Anne's equestrian expertise can be compared with that of Elizabeth, Empress of Austria. It was obvious that if she was to be happily married her husband must be a horseman of note.

Princess Anne was fourteen when she first achieved a clear round over seven fences, against nineteen other competitors. She was introduced to Mark Phillips at a competitors' party after the Eridge Horse Trials.

In 1968, when the British team won a gold medal at the Mexico Olympics, Mark Phillips was the youngest-ever reserve rider, and when he and the Princess met at the celebrations on their return, there was no mistaking their admiration for each other.

It was on what would have been the Queen Mother's fiftieth wedding anniversary that Prince Philip announced 'among ourselves' Princess Anne's engagement.

They were married in November 1973.

HM KING LEKA I OF ALBANIA
& MISS SUSAN CULLEN-WARD

1975

Son of the flamboyant King Zog, King Leka was born in Albania and left his country three days later in the arms of his mother.

He lived with his family in England during the war, then in Alexandria at the invitation of King Farouk of Egypt before moving to Madrid. Leka was proclaimed King in 1961 in the Hotel Bristol in Paris in the presence of a hastily convened temporary National Assembly.

In 1975 King Leka fell in love with an attractive fair-haired Australian girl, the daughter of a sheep-farmer, who is now known as Queen Susan. They were married in Biarritz amid scenes of loyalty from Albanian monarchists.

Susan became the first Australian Queen anywhere, and her husband is fortunately very rich as his father brought his huge fortune out of Albania.

King Leka is very intelligent and well-read, and he also has the fighting spirit of the Albanians and the progressive drive and determination of his father.

His dream is to return home and rule over his small mountainous country.

HM KING CARL XVI GUSTAF OF SWEDEN
& MISS SILVIA SOMMERLATH

1976

'Something went "click" in my mind,' the King said, 'and it was love at first sight.'

The young King was attending the Munich Olympics in 1972 when he met Silvia Sommerlath, who was acting as principal hostess to visiting VIPs.

King Carl came to the throne in 1973. He is a keen yachtsman, a skilled scuba driver and water-skier. He is also a cross-country skier, while fencing and swimming are among his other sports. He is particularly interested in technical research and material science, while Silvia had specialized in languages and graduated at the University of Düsseldorf.

The marriage took place at Stockholm in June 1976, and the menu for the wedding breakfast at the Castle included Scottish woodpigeon.

The bride wore a unique diadem of cameos set in red gold with pearls, which had previously belonged to King Carl's mother.

The Marriage took place in Sweden in 1976 and there was a Royal Procession through the streets of Stockholm in an open carriage to the Cathedral. Afterwards the Bride and Bridegroom sailed in a barge to the Royal Palace where the Reception was held. Lining the streets was a crowd of 180,000 and more than five million watched on television.

HRH PRINCE MICHAEL OF KENT
& BARONESS MARIE-CHRISTINE VON REIBNITZ
1978

Shy, quiet and retiring, Prince Michael was little known to the public until he fell in love with the beautiful, clever and talented Marie-Christine von Reibnitz.

They had great difficulty in getting married because the Baroness had been married to an Englishman, and divorced by mutual consent. As a devout Catholic she had to have an annulment in order to marry again.

Prince Michael had to renounce his rights of succession to the throne, because he was marrying a Catholic, although any children of the marriage still retain them as Anglicans.

Everything was arranged and the Queen had

Neither the disappointments nor the setbacks could dim the happiness and joy which radiated from the bride and groom.

given her consent when, in June 1978, the Pope refused to grant Prince Michael a dispensation to marry. Marie-Christine was very unhappy as this dispensation had been granted before in such cases.

Amidst the furore Prince Michael and Marie-Christine went on planning their wedding for the last day in June.

A civil service took place in the Town Hall in Vienna in the presence of twenty close relatives, as had been planned, but the religious ceremony had to be reduced to a simple Mass instead of a wedding ceremony.

After all the obstacles and difficulties Prince and Princess Michael of Kent are blissfully happy. She is adored by the public. Her *joie de vivre* is infectious and her charm has captivated everyone who meets her.

Prince Michael has left the army and is now starting a business career.

They have a son, Lord Frederick Windsor, and a daughter, Gabriela, born in April 1981.

HRH The Prince of Wales
& The Lady Diana Spencer
1981

123

...and they lived happily ever after.

INDEX OF NAMES

Albany, Duke of, 19
Albert I, Prince of Monaco, 67
Albert, Prince of Saxe-Coburg, 46, 47, 48
Albert Victor, Prince, 69
Alexander I, King of Bulgaria, 66
Alexander I, King of Greece, 77
Alexander II, Tsar, 64, 65
Alexandra, Princess of Greece, 77
Alexandra, Princess of Hesse, 71
Alfonso XII, King of Spain, 63
Algiers, Cardinal Lavigérie, Archbishop of, 61
Algiers, Dey of, 28
Amsberg, Claus von, 106, 107
Angevins, family of, 11
Angoulême, Audemar, Count of, 10
Anne, Princess, 113
Aragon, Dona Fabiola de Mora y, 97
Aragon, Katharine of, 16, 17
Armstrong-Jones, Antony, later Earl of Snowdon, 99
Augustus, Prince of Saxony, 25
Augustus the Strong, King of Saxony, 25
Ayesha, Princess of Cooch Behar, 88, 89

Baldwin, Mrs Stanley, 87
Barcelona, Count of, 102
Bath, family of, 9
Battenberg, family of, 50
Baudouin, King of the Belgians, 97
Beatrix, Princess, later Queen, of the Netherlands, 106, 107
Beauharnais, Josephine de, 36, 37, 59
Beauharnais, Vicomte de, 36
Boleyn, Anne, 16, 17
Boleyn, Mary, 16
Bonaparte, Caroline, later Queen of Naples, 38
Bonaparte, Napoleon, Emperor of France, 36, 37, 38
Bothwell, Earl of, 19
Bowes-Lyon, Lady Elizabeth, 78
Brignole, Catherine de, 26
Buggin, Lady Cecilia, 35

Canute, King, 9
Carl XIV Gustaf, King of Sweden, 119
Carol II, King of Roumania, 94
Catherine the Great, Empress of Russia, 27
Catherine Mikhailova, Grand Duchess of Russia, 50
Charles, Archduke, 15
Charles, Prince of Wales, 122
Charlotte, Princess, 41
Constantine, King of Greece, 102
Constantin, Grand Duke of Russia, 58
Cooke, Hope, 103
Cullen-Ward, Susan, later queen, 117

Darnley, Earl of, 19
Digby, Jane, 56, 57

Dolgornky, Princess Catherine, 64, 65
Douglas-Hamilton, Lady Mary, 67
Dubucq, Aimée, 28, 29
Dysart, family of, 9

Edward I, 11
Edward VIII, 87
Eleanor of Aquitaine, 10
Eleanor of Castile, 12
Elisabeth, Duchess in Bavaria, 54, 55
Elizabeth, Princess, 17
Elizabeth, Princess, later Queen, of England, 90
Emma, Queen, 8
Ernst August, Prince of Hanover, 75
Essex, Earl of, 10
Ethelred the Unready, 11
Eulalia, Princess, 63

Fairbrother, John, 49
Fairbrother, Louisa, 49
Fernando VIII, King of Spain, 42
Ferdinand, Prince of Saxe-Coburg, 45
FitzHerbert, Mrs Maria, 30, 31
Flanders, Baldwin V, Count of, 9
Francis, King of France, 15
François, Dauphin of France, 19
Franz Joseph, Emperor of Austria, 54, 55
Frederick, Crown Prince of Denmark, 59

Genoa, Doge of, 26
George III, 34
George I, King of Greece, 58
Granville, family of, 9

Hamilton, Duke of, 67
Harald, Crown Prince of Norway, 110
Haraldsen, Sonja, 110
Hauke, Countess Julie von, 50, 51
Heine, Alice, 67
Helen, Princess of Greece, 94
Hélène, Duchess in Bavaria, 54
Henry Plantagenet, 10
Hitler, Adolf, 94
Honoré III, Prince of Monaco, 26

India, Shah Jehan, Emperor of, 21
Indira, Princess of Baroda, 76
Isabella of Aquitaine, 10, 11
Isobelle of Gloucester, 10

Jaipur, Maharaja of, 88, 89
Jaipur, Maharani of, 88
João VI, King of Portugal, 45
Johann I, King of Saxony, 73
John, King, 10, 11
Juan Carlos, Prince, later King, of Spain, 102
Juliana, Queen of the Netherlands, 106

Kelly, Grace, 95
Kent, Princess Alexandra of, 108

Kent, Prince George, Duke of, 54, 55
Kent, Princess Marina, Duchess of, 84
Kent, Prince Michael of, 120, 121

Lallah Yamma, 61
Lansdowne, family of, 9
Leka I, King of Albania, 117
Leopold, Prince of Saxe-Coburg, 41
Loisinger, Louise, 66
Louis III, Grand Duke, 51
Louis XII, King of France, 15
Louis XIV, King of France, 26, 27
Louise, Crown Princess of Saxony, 73
Louise, Princess of Sweden and Norway, 59
Ludovika, Duchess in Bavaria, 54
Ludwig I, King, 56
Lupescu, Elena, 94
Lusignan, Hugh IX, Lord of, 10

Mahal, Begum Mumtaz, 21
Mahmoud, 29
Maintenon, Madame de, 26, 27
Manos, Aspasia, 77
Maria Cristina, Queen Regent of Spain, 42, 43
Maria de Gloria, Queen of Portugal, 45
Maria Josepha, Archduchess, 25
Margaret, Princess, 99
Margrethe, Princess, later Queen, of Denmark, 109
Mary, Queen of Scots, 19
Mary Tudor, Duchess of Suffolk, 15
Matilda of Flanders, 8, 9
Maximilian, Duke in Bavaria, 54
May, Princess of Teck, 68, 69
Mercedes, Dona Maria de las, 63
Messell, Oliver, 99
Mezrab, Shiek Abd ul Medjuel el, 56, 57
Miguel, Dom, 45
Monpezat, Count Henri, later Prince Henrik, de, 107
Montijo, Eugénie de, 52, 53
Mountbatten, family of, 50
Mountbatten of Burma, Earl, 90
Mountbatten, Philip, later Duke of Edinburgh, 90
Muñoz, Fernando, later duke of Riansares, 42, 43
Murat, André, 38
Murat, Joachim, later King of Naples, 38
Murray, Lady Augusta, 34, 35

Naksh, 28
Napoleon III, Emperor of France, 52, 53
Nicholas II, Tsar, 71
Normandy, Duke of, 9
Nicholas, Prince of Greece, 82, 84

Ogilvy, Angus, 108
Olga, Princess of Greece, 58
Otto, King of Greece, 57

Pallikares, 57
Paul, King of Greece, 102
Paul, Prince of Yugoslavia, 82
Pedro, Emperor of Brazil, Dom, 45
Pembroke, Marquis of, 17
Peter the Great, 27
Piccard, Aurélie, 60, 61
Phillips, Captain Mark,
Potemkin, Prince Gregory, 27

Rainier III, Prince of Monaco, 95
Reibnitz, Baroness Marie-Christine
    von, 120, 121
Rizzio, David, 19
Rollo, Duke of Normandy, 9

Schwarzenberg, Prince Felix, 56
Sikkim, Maharaj-Prince of, 103
Simpson, Mrs Wallis, 87

Sofia, Princess of Greece, 102
Sophie, Archduchess of Austria, 55
Sommerlath, Silvia, 119
Spencer, family of, 9
Spencer, Lady Diana, 122
Steenacker, Madame, 61
Strathmore, Lady, 78
Suffolk, Charles Brandon, Duke of, 15
Sussex, Prince Augustus, Duke of, 34,
    35
Sutherland, family of, 9

Tedjani, Prince Si Ahmed, 60, 61
Theotoky, Count Spyridon, 56
Turkey, Abd ul Hamid, Sultan of, 28,
    29

Venningen, Baron Carl-Theodore von,
    56

Viktoria Luise, Princess of Prussia, 75
Victoria, Queen, 45, 46, 47, 48, 49
Vera, Grand Duchess of Russia, 58

Wales, Prince of, later George IV, 30,
    31
Windsor, Lord Frederick, 121
William the Conqueror, 8, 9
William of Glücksberg, 58
Worsley, Katharine, 100
Worsley, Sir William, 100

Yurievsky, Princess, 64
York, Prince Albert, later George VI,
    Duke of, 78
York, Prince George, later George V,
    Duke of, 68, 69

ACKNOWLEDGEMENTS

The author and publishers wish to thank the following for permission to reproduce photographs and illustrations:

ANP-Foto, page 107 (t, bl, br)
Ashmolean Museum, Oxford, page 57 (b)
BBC Hulton Picture Library, pages 27 (b), 35, 51 (l), 58 (b), 76, 82 and 83 (tl, b)
Beadle and Cooper, page 122 (r)
Trustees of Bedford Estate, page 14
Lesley Blanch, page 64
British Museum, London, pages 8 (t) and 15
Camera Press, pages 87 (r), 90 (l, r), 92 (t), 93 (tr), 108, 109 (l, tr, br), 110 (tl, r), 111, 112, 113 (t), 115, 116, 120 (t), 121 (tl, b), 123 (r) and 126 (l, r)
Central Press, pages 79 (t, bl, br), 84, 85 (tl, b), 87 (l), 91 (t, b), 95 (b), 98, 99 (l), 102 (l, r), 113 (bl,br), 117 (r) and 125 (cl, tr, br)
Cooper-Bridgeman Library, pages 24 (t), 48 (b) and 54 (t)
Copyright Reserved, page 32 (b)
Daily Telegraph Colour Library, page 114 (b)
Mary Evans Picture Library, pages 9 (b), 10 (l, r), 12 (l, r), 17 (t), 18 (br), 27 (tr), 31 (b), 37 (tr), 45 (t), 53 (tl, b), 55 (tr), 59 (br), 71 (tl, r) and 72 (br)
Fox Photos, pages 96, 97 (tl, tr, b), 104, 105 (l) and 122 (l)
Giraudon, pages 23 (l), 24 (b), 27 (tl), 36 (l, r), 37 (l, br), 38 (l, r), 39, 47 (r), 52 (l, r) and 65 (l)
Roger Hall, pages 25, 26, 42, 44, 50 and 60
Sonia Halliday, pages 28 (l) and 61
Robert Harding Associates, pages 11 and 17 (b)
Michael Holford, pages 8 (b), 9 (t), 13 (tl), 20, 21, 23 (tl, b) and 45 (b)
Angelo Hornak, page 67 (b)
Keystone Press, pages 88 (t, b), 103 (tl, tr, b), 121 (tr) and 123 (l)

MacQuitty Collection, page 89 (t)
Mander and Mitchenson Theatre Collection, page 49 (l)
Mansell Collection, pages 19 (t), 31 (t), 32 (t), 49 (r), 54 (b), 55 (br), 58 (tl, tr), 59 (l, tr), 66 (l, r), 70, 72 (t, bl), 74, 75 and 77 (r)
Francis Marshall, page 57 (t) and 94
MAS, pages 43 (t, b), 62 and 63 (l)
National Portrait Gallery, London, pages 16 (r), 19 (b), 30, 33 (bl), 34 (t), 40, 41 (l), 81 (tr) and 86
National Trust, page 18 (t)
Novosti Press Agency, page 65 (br)
Picturepoint, page 13 (tr, bl, br)
Paul Popper, pages 28 (r), 53 (tr), 55 (l), 65 (tr), 71 (b), 73 (l, r), 77 (l), 78, 80 (t, b), 81 (tl, b), 83 (tr), 92 (b), 93 (tl, b), 95 (t), 99 (r), 100, 101, 105 (r), 106 and 110 (b)
Rex Features, pages 85 (tr), 114 (t), 118, 119 (t, bl, br), 120 (b), 124 (t, bl, bc, br) and 125 (tl, bl)
The Royal Pavilion, Art Gallery and Museums, Brighton, page 33 (br)
Salmer, page 29 (b)
Scala, page 22
Scottish National Portrait Gallery, page 18 (bl)
Snark, page 41 (r)
Sotheby, Parke, Bernet and Co, page 34 (b)
SUS, page 117 (l)
Collection Baron Karl von Venningen, page 56
Victoria and Albert Museum, page 29 (t)
Wallace Collection, page 33 (t)
Zefa, page 63 (r)

The pictures on pages 16 (l), 46, 47 (l), 48 (t) and 69 are reproduced by Gracious Permission of Her Majesty the Queen.